AUSTRALIAN NATURE
In Poetry

Margot Petersen

Partly Illustrated by TED BRAMBLEBY BSC Marine Biologist

Table of Contents

3. Acknowledgements

4. Introduction

5. Billabong

6. Mt Warning

7. Bushland

8. Cormorant

9. Dusk

10. Dawn

11. Spider

12. Sweet Awakenings

13. Tide

14. Bassie

15. Kingfisher

16. Uninvited Guest

17. Magpie

18. Goanna

19. Oyster Catcher

20. Spoonbill

21. Tweed River

22. Pandanus

23. Dunes

24. Driftwood

25. Gorge

26. She Oak

27. Secret Pond

28. Pelican

29. Half a Boat

30. Kookaburra

31. Ibis

32. Plovers

33. Curlew

34. Gecko

35. Egret

36. Bush Turkey

37. Butcher Bird

38. Cicada

39. Lucky

40. Wobbegong

41. Rainbow Lorikeet

42. Rain

43. Hidden Danger

Acknowledgements

Dedicated to my Daughter Lise who brings constant joy to my life & who was the inspiration for some of these poems.

Ronnie Rankin - Foyer Printing. My good friend, without whose help in it's production, this book would probably not have reached this stage!

Ted Brambleby - BSC Marine Biologist. For his unique & beautiful illustrations & knowledgeable professional input. Ted's illustrations all bear his signature.

Kirrilly Barnard and Heather Gillard - Graphic Artists, Foyer Printing. For their imaginative & professional help in the layout of this book.

Sandra Fryer. My friend who deciphered & promptly typed the first draft of this book from my original, sometimes hastily scribbled manuscript.

Introduction

This collection of poems reflects on the local wildlife I have had the pleasure of interacting with over the last 15 years.

I live in a small far Northern NSW Australian coastal village where my home backs onto an estuarine creek and fronts onto the Pacific Ocean with just a strip of bushland separating them.

I go to sleep to the sound of the ocean and wake to the sounds of the creatures that feature in my poems.

I do not claim to be an expert on wildlife and my poems are based on my observations over time and the subjects traits with which I have become most familiar. All of the places I mention are real and are within a 10minute walk except for Mt Warning and the Tweed River which are within a 20 minute drive.

Any of the Facts I provide have been carefully researched, or provided to me by a highly respected local Marine Biologist whose love of nature far exceeds my own. I think adults will find them informative and children educational. He has also generously assisted me with many of my illustrations and I am extremely grateful for this and his well informed input.

It is hoped my poems may be enjoyed by people of all ages and have included a little touch of humour in some that I think might appeal to the younger generation in particular.

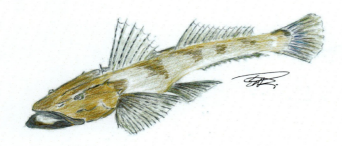

Billabong

Billabongs are usually formed when the path of a creek or river changes, leaving the former branch with a dead end. They fill with water seasonally and are dry for the rest of the year. The word billabong is probably derived from the indigenous term "bilaban". Coolabah trees usually grow along the banks of the billabong.

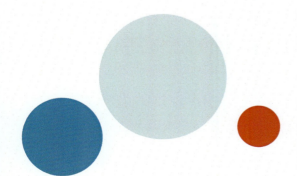

There's a place that I go to
When life goes wrong
It's a place that I call
My own Billabong

When the rain falls heavy
Its banks overflow
When the drought hits
Its heart beats slow

It's a place of serenity
of relief from all tension
As I gaze at its waters
And the Coolabah's reflection

Mt Warning

On 17th May 1770 Lieutenant James Cook saw a mountain from the sea. To warn others that came after him he named it Mt Warning.

It is the central volcanic remnant of the Tweed Volcano that would have been 1900m (6,200') above sea level, almost twice the height of the current mountain.

This volcano erupted 23 million years ago. It is a place of traditional significance to the Bundjalung people and is the sight of particular ceremonies and initiation rites.

Due to Mt Warning's proximity to Cape Byron the Australian Continent's Eastern most point it is the first place on mainland Australia to receive the sun's rays each day. Over 60,000 people a year make the 4.4km, five hour round trip trek to the top from Breakfast Creek.

Like a sentinel guarding the land
Stands Mount Warning
The sun's first rays
Kiss your peak each morning

You cast your shadow
Over river and field
And bestow your blessings
On the crops that they yield

Whether towering above
Or viewed from afar
Your craggy peak
Is a landmark spectacular

Your grey silhouette
Against a blue sky
Constantly pops into view
For travellers nearby

Most days your crag
Stands bold and proud
Occasionally it sulks
Behind a low lying cloud

Those brave enough
To scale your height
Are rewarded with a view
Their soul to delight

Bushland

There is a bushland that beckons
On the far side of the creek
I would like to explore it
But its banks are too steep

So I go there in my mind
And imagine the critters that I think
Live in the bushland
On the far side of the creek

In its burrows would be
Bandicoots and wombats and rabbits
and hares
In the branches of its gumtrees
Would be sleepy koala bears

In its grasses there would be
All sorts of wrigglies me thinks

There would be lizards and snakes
And goannas and geckos and skinks

In its trees there would be
Butcherbirds and magpies and
currawongs too
There would be laughing kookaburras
And black and white cockatoos

If you're very, very lucky
And very patient too
If you waited long enough
You might spot a kangaroo

These are the critters
In my mind that I think
Live in the bushland
On the far side of the creek.

Cormorant

All cormorants are fish eaters dining on small eels, fish and even water snakes.
Under water they propel themselves with their feet. Sometimes diving to depths as much as 45m. After fishing cormorants go ashore and are frequently seen holding their wings out to the sun to dry.

The cormorant has
Amazing ability
Not many fish
Can escape his agility

When he ducks under water
Intending to sup
You never know where
He will next pop up

When he spreads his wings
To dry in the air
He almost looks
Like a bird in prayer

Dusk

Dusk is that quiet
Time of the day
When its trials and tribulations
Slowly fade away

As I raise my eye
To the darkening sky
The Evening Star
Is the first to rise

For those who voyage
On the oceans wide
Its shining light
Will become their guide.

Dawn

As I walk on an empty beach at dawn
I feel the fresh breeze of an autumn morn
A crescent moon lingers in a velvet sky
And one lonely star shimmers nearby

It feels like it is
Just we three
A lingering crescent moon
A lonely star and me

Then as the sun begins to rise
And take possession of the morning skies
I hear the sound of a bird's first song
And the lingering crescent moon and the star
are gone.

Spider

The main group of modern spiders first appeared in the Triassic period, 200million years ago. All species are predators, mostly preying on insects and other spiders. Spiders' guts are too narrow to take solids and they liquidise their food by flooding it with digestive enzymes. Although most spiders live for 2 years at most, Tarantulas can live up to 25 years in captivity.

Spider spider spinning your web
With all the skill of an engineer
You can be seen summer nights
As the sun disappears.

Your patience is endless
All the night long
As all sorts of insects
To your web throng.

You don't order pizza
There is no need
One careless fly
Will provide a good feed.

You don't have a mortgage
And you don't pay rent
And you can take your house with you
When the night is spent.

Sweet Awakenings

There is a magpie that
wakes me each day
He tunefully prods me
To get things underway

Sometimes I would like
To linger in bed
But he's got different ideas
In his black & white head

He's there summer and winter
Every day without fail
In sunshine or rain
In storm sleet or hail

It's a most pleasant way
To be woken each day
It beats an alarm clock
Tingling away

I don't have to set him
He charges no fee
He's Nature's alarm clock
Pearched in a tree.

Tide

The unique ecosystem found in the intricate mesh of mangroves roots offers a quiet marine region for young organisms including algae, barnacles & oysters, all of which require a hard surface for anchoring while they filter feed.
Shrimp & mud lobsters use the muddy bottoms as their home. Despite restoration efforts developers & others have removed over half of the worlds mangroves in recent times.

I stand on the bank
Of an estuarine creek
As the tide coming in
Reaches its peak

Still bearing spume
From the ocean green
It makes its way
To places upstream

Ripple by ripple
Surge by surge
It slowly creeps up
To the mangrove's verge

Two times a day
It will ebb and flow
And in the safety of its waters
Marine life will grow.

Bassie

Bass also known as the Freshwater Perch can grow 1kg to 4kg depending on available food.
Often found upstream in freshwater, prefers cover such as timber or rocky outcrop.
May be found in still pools or fast running streams.

There was a fish called Bassie
He belonged to a man named Ted
Every night Ted fed him
And saw him safely to bed.

His home was an aquarium
There he thrived and dwelt
And shared many secrets
With the man named Ted.

In his small world he lived and played
He was happy, loved and cherished
Right up until the fateful day
He so sadly perished.

Bassie had a bad habit
Of jumping way too high
And alas on one unlucky Day
He jumped right out and died

So Ted built for him a little boat
And sent him out on an evening tide
Now Bassie swims forever
On the Rivers wide.

Kingfisher

Kingfishers hunt from an exposed perch from which they swoop on their prey to snatch it and then return to their perch. Having beaten the prey it is manipulated and swallowed.

Most species have bright plumage with little difference between the sexes. All have large heads, sharp pointed bills, short legs and stubby tails. The plumage of most kingfishers is bright with green and blue being the most common colours.

Kingfisher your colour is so brilliant
With your electric patch of blue
But it is not always easy
To cast my eye on you

You probably will be sitting still
On a branch hanging over the creek
Looking for your supper
In the water still but deep

I have not ever heard you sing
You probably have no need
Your beauty is in your feathers hue
With your electric patch of blue.

Uninvited **Guest**

Long nose for digging long
conical tunnels in backyards
and heathland along
Australia's East Coast.
Daytime is spent in a grass
and leaf lined nest.
They forage for food at night,
mostly solitary. Food includes
insects, insect larvae (grubs),
bulbs and tubers.

We were having pizza
In the backyard one night
When someone came to join us
Without waiting for an invite

He sat there looking at us
As we enjoyed our meal
Then he suddenly decided
A piece of it to steal

He was brown and furry
And not a bit shy
When he took our loot
What a cheeky uninvited little
bandicoot.

Magpie

The Australian Magpie is closely
related to the butcherbird.
It is one of Australia's most
accomplished songbirds and has an
array of complex vocalisations.
It walks rather than hops and spends
much time on the ground.

Magpie all dressed up
In his suit of black and white
In the trees of my garden
He's a most welcome sight

We all should know
It is best to steer clear
As breeding time approaches
Around Spring of each year

He will swoop out of nowhere
And peck you on the head
So a broad brimmed hat
Will stand you in good stead

For this unpleasant trait
He will soon be forgiven
When he sings his tuneful song
You will again be smitten.

Goanna

A goanna is a swift mover and when pressed, will sprint short distances on its hind legs.
Its prey can include small animals, insects, smaller lizards, snakes, mammals, birds and eggs.
They are wary of human intrusions into their habitat and will most likely run away if confronted.

There is a fat goanna
Who comes to visit me
When the other critters spy him
They very quickly flee

He postures aggressively
As he stomps boldly around
Confidently taking possession
Of all that does surround

But I suspect he is not
As brave as he appears
I sometimes think he's bluffing
To scare away his peers.

Oyster Catcher

All oyster catchers have bright orange-red bill, eye-rings and legs and red eyes.
It is found in coastal areas throughout the Australian Continent.
The current population may be as low as 10,000.
They feed on bivalve molluscs, which are prised apart with their specially adapted bills.

There's a pair of oyster catchers
They live on a nearby rocky shore
I see them each morning
Just after the dawn

Bright red beaks
Make them easy to spot
As they shyly graze
Among oyster clad rocks

If you happen to come across them
Treat them with great care
'cause there are not many left
In the world to share.

Spoonbill

Spoonbills have large, flat, spetulate
bills and feed by wading through
shallow water, sweeping the partly
open bill from side to side.
They need to feed many hours
a day.
They are monogamous but only for
one season at a time.

The spoonbill is the hoover
Of the creek
As he scours the mangroves
With his long blunt beak

His head moves quickly
From side to side
As he searches for crustaceans
That in the sand hide

Then he will retrace his steps
Head still going side to side
Searching for other tasty morsels
On the incoming tide.

Tweed River

Tweed River was discovered by European explorer John Oxley in 1823.

The river rises on the Eastern slopes of the Great Dividing Range and flows generally north -east, joined by the Oxley and Rous Rivers before reaching its mouth at its confluence with the South Pacific Ocean descending 173 metres over its 78km course.

On its journey it passes through the urban centres of Murwillumbah and Tweed Heads and the village of Tumbulgum.

The lowlands along the river are used for farming, sugar cane and other crops.

The traditional custodians of the land surrounding the Tweed River are the Aboriginal people of the Minjungbal Clan.

Mighty Tweed River broad deep and green
You carve through the land
on your way to the sea
The sights on your banks
changing endlessly

Farmlets and small villages
And crops of sugar cane
Cling to your banks
And thrive in your domain

You have given of your bounty
To the Natives of the land
Before surrendering your waters
To the ocean and sand

Pandanus

Pandanus grow wild throughout the tropical and subtropical Pacific, where they withstand strong winds, drought and salt spray.
Pandanus is one of the iconic tree genera of the North Coast of NSW.

Pandanus are my favourite plant
I could not love them more
And in my little part of the world
They dominate the shore

They thrive on dunes and headlands
Often buffered by strong winds
Whatever nature throws at them
They cope due to pliant limbs

They have epitomised the beach to me
Ever since I was a child
It seems to me wherever there's a beach
You will see them growing wild

Dunes

A dune is a hill of sand built either by wind or water flow.
They run parallel to the shoreline, directly inland from the beach.
The dunes protect the land against invasion of stormwater from the ocean.
Dune habitats provide niches for highly specialised plants and wildlife.

Dunes stretching endlessly
Are nature's buffer between land and sea
Only spinafex holds you together
Ever so tenuously

In wild stormy weather
The ocean may rob you of your sand
Causing you to crumble
And deplete the coastal land

Given time King Neptune
Will repay his debt
And the universal clock of nature
Will once again be set.

Driftwood

Driftwood is wood that has been washed onto a beach by the action of winds, tides or waves.

It provides shelter and food for the birds and aquatic species as it floats in the ocean.

When the partially decomposed wood washes ashore it can shelter birds and plants and eventually become the foundation for sand dunes.

Driftwood on the beach
You will find
Smoothed and contorted
By time and tide

It will tell you many secrets
If you listen carefully
Of things that have been
And of things that might be

It will tell you
Of many things it has seen
And it will tell you
Of many things you might see.

Gorge

Bamboo sharks are relatively small. The largest species reach no more than 121cm (48 in) in adult body length. They have elongated bodies with unusually long tails which exceed the length of the fish and feed off bottom dwelling invertebrates and smaller fish.

There's a gorge at the base
Of a rocky headland
Where crystal clear waters
Caress pristine sand

In its shallow depths
Bamboo sharks dwell
And swim idly
'neath the ocean's swell

If you're brave enough to join them
They will eye you curiously
As they share their domain
In an azure sea.

She Oak

She oaks are endemic to Australia occurring primarily in the south. They are notable for their long, segmented branchlets that function as leaves. Because of its ability to thrive in very poor soil and to completely cover the ground with its needles, it is often used to stabilise sand dunes.

A she oak clings
To sands of a dune
And whispers its story
To an ocean breeze

It tells of two lovers
Who used tryst in its shade
And of the promises
To each other they made

It tells of a box
That he buried in the sand
And in it secretly left for her
A golden wedding band.

Secret Pond

There's a secret pond
That lies behind the dunes
And on its still surface
Lilac water lilies bloom

I think I'm the only one
Who knows it is there
When I sit on its banks
My soul to repair

Dragonflies skim past silently
And they are all
That I need
To keep me company.

Pelican

Fossil evidence of pelicans dates back 30 million years. Pelicans frequent coastal and inland waters where they feed principally on fish, catching them at or near the waters surface.

They use thermals for soaring to heights of 3000m (10,000') combined with gliding and commutes distances of up to 150km to feeding areas.

The pelican is a very special bird
His landings magnificent
His take-offs absurd

He walks on land with ungainly waddle
But his grace in the air as he glides to
the heights
Is one of nature's
Most wonderful sights

He instinctively knows
Where food is most plentiful
And travels great distances
To ensure a big belly full.

Half a Boat

I have the remains
Of half a boat
It's a long, long time
Since it has been afloat

I first saw it lying
In the yard next door
And t'was given to me
'cause t'was wanted no more

It has been transported
To four new homes
And with each move
The more it creaks and groans

One thing's for sure
Wherever I roam
My half boat will come
With me to my next home.

Kookaburra

Kookabrras are terrestrial tree kingfishers native to Australia and New Guinea. It is one of the largest of the kingfisher family.

Their prey is seized by pouncing from a suitable perch. Small prey is eaten whole, but large prey is killed by bashing it against the ground or a tree branch.

They are believed to pair for life. Usually offspring of the previous one or two years act as "helpers" and during breeding season every bird in the group shares all parenting duties.

Kookaburra kookaburra ka ka ka
You seem to be happiest
When the grounds not too far

You don't choose to soar
Like lesser birds do
Life closer to earth
Is the one that suits you

You gracefully swoop
From tree to tree
As you eye the ground
For a wriggling delicacy.

Ibis

The white ibis usually gives off a foul stench.
Its call is a long croak.
It is sometimes considered a problem because of its scavenging habits.
They are even known to snatch sandwiches from picnicker's hands.
Their most favourite food is crayfish and mussels which it obtains by digging with its long bill.
It can soar to great heights.

The ibis is not
A very pretty bird
With his great curved beak
He looks quite absurd

But don't be fooled
He's a very clever guy
And can reach great heights
In the azure sky

His scavenging habits
Verge on a sin
And don't be surprised
If he opens your bin.

Plovers

Since plovers live on the ground they always alert and even though it rests it never really sleeps. They have a loud range of calls, a warning call, a loud defending call, courtship calls, calls to its young and others.
They are best known for their bold nesting habits on any stretch of open ground including suburban parks, school ovals and even supermarket carparks and flat rooftops.
Nesting pairs defend their territory by calling loudly, spreading their wings and then swooping fast and low on intruders.

Mr and Mrs Plover
Make great mums and dads
But they are not very careful
Where they build their pads

Their choice of nesting place
Is not always discreet
And is often on the edge
Of a very busy street

They tend to breed
About twice a year
And suddenly
Four fluffy chicks appear

They grow very quickly
After they arrive
But sadly
Probably only one will survive

They forage all over
The neighbourhood
Often stopping to rest
On just one foot

The chicks run to safety
In times of bad weather
And nestle cosily
Under mum and dad's feathers.

Curlew

The beach stone curlew is a large ground dwelling bird endemic to Australia.

It is mainly nocturnal and forages individually or in pairs over a large home range, particularly on moonlit nights. When disturbed they freeze motionless. This works well as a defence against visual predators.

It is probably heard more than it is seen. Its call sounds like a wail or a scream in the night.

When scared it screeches.

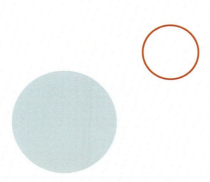

In the dead of the night
When all is still
I am sometimes woken
By the curlew's mournful shrill

He is not often seen
During the day
He comes out at night
Seeking his prey

As I lie in my bed
With an open eye
I wonder what it is
That makes the curlew cry.

Gecko

Geckos use chirping sounds to interact with other geckos.
Most cannot blink and often lick their eyes to keep them clean and moist. They are usually nocturnal and are great climbers and can cross indoor ceilings with ease.

Shy little gecko hiding
In my house somewhere
If it wasn't for your chirp, chirp, chirp
I would never know you're there

Walking upside down on the ceiling
To you is no mean feat
Nature made it easy
By giving you webbed feet

And if it sometime happens
That we accidentally meet
You quickly scurry off
On those tiny webbed feet

Egret

The egret feeds in shallow water mainly on fish, frogs, small reptiles and insects spearing them with its long sharp bill.
It will often wait motionless for prey or slowly stalks its victim.

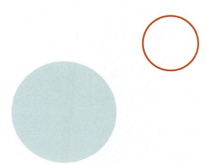

Egret walking gracefully
Along the creek
Waiting to lunge
With his long pointed beak

He silently stalks
The incoming tide
Searching for his prey
That in its waters hide

He will stand like a statue
Till the time is just right
For some unsuspecting fish
With his beak to strike.

Brush Turkey

Brush turkeys use the same nesting site year after year.
Up to 50 eggs laid by several females may be found in a single mound.
The eggs are favourite food for goannas, snakes and dingoes.
The newly hatched young dig themselves out of the mound and then have to take care of themselves.
They will nest in suburban gardens and will patiently remove enormous amounts of mulch from neighbouring gardens.

Brush turkeys watch very carefully
While their eggs are incubating
Always checking nest temperatures
Are the parents in waiting

But from the minute his egg hatches
He is on his own
No help from mum or dad
Is this guy shown

He learns very early
It's the quick or the dead
When it comes dinner time
As to who gets fed

He 'll dig up your garden
At the blink of an eye
And then build a great mound
In the middle of your drive

He really is a nuisance
In so many ways
But I still like to watch him roosting
At the end of the day.

Butcherbird

Butcherbirds get their name from their habit of impaling prey on a thorn or tree fork.
This is used to store prey for later consumption, or to attract mates. They have high pitched complex songs, which are used to defend their year-round group territories.

The butcherbird sometimes
Sings for her supper
Her range is amazing
From lower to upper

She sometimes stores her food
In the fork of a tree
Hoping to attract
A hungry husband to be

If you're very lucky
And wait patiently
She just might reward you
With a tuneful melody

From a trill to a warble
She'll go through the whole scale
And the very next morning
She'll be back without fail.

Cicada

Many people around the world regularly eat cicadas.
The name cicada is derived from the Latin cicada meaning "tree cricket". Some cicadas produce sounds up to 120db, among the loudest of all insect-produced sounds, and is loud enough to cause permanent hearing loss in humans should the cicada sing just outside the listener's ear. They live underground for most of their lives (up to 17 years) as nymphs sucking sap from various trees.

Lazy cicada you spend most of your life
Living under the ground
And during this time
You do not make a sound

In summer the bush
Comes alive with your song
As you hum on and off
All the day long

Your shrillness can make
The inner ear quiver
If one stands too close
As your chant you deliver

But your voice is loudest
On a hot summer night
When the other bush critters
Have all gone quiet.

Lucky

I have a cat named Lucky
She has a mind of her own
She does not act like other cats
She totally walks alone

She does not mind when a currawong
constantly pecks at her food
She just sits & watches him
And refuses to intrude

The currawong is pushing his luck
I have a sneaking hunch
Lucky just might change her mind
And gobble him up for lunch.

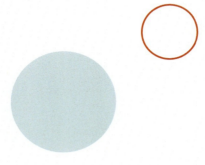

Wobbegong

Wobbegong is the common name given to 12 species of carpet sharks. The are bottom dwelling sharks and spend much of their time resting on the sea floor. They hide among rocks and catch smaller fish which swim to close. Wobbegongs are generally not dangerous to humans unless they are provoked. They may bite scuba divers or snorkellers who poke or touch them. They have small sharp teeth. Having once bitten they may hang on and can be very difficult to remove.

Under a shelf in a rock pool
On a rocky shore
A fat lazy Wobbegong
Dwells on the ocean floor

I have not seen him for myself
Ted told me of his lair
Ted is a friend of mine
Who often snorkels there

He does not need
To go out to dine
The passing smorgasbord
Fills his needs just fine

He can choose from
Lobster, octopus, prawns galore
Nature delivers it free of charge
Fresh to his front door

Rainbow Lorikeet

With its colourful plumage & bright red beak the rainbow lorikeet is unmistakable. Both sexes have a blue head & belly with green wings. It is common along the Eastern seaboard of Australia from Northern Queensland to South Australia. Its habitat is coastal bushland, rainforest & woodland. In many suburban gardens wild lorikeets are used to humans and can be hand fed. They chase off not only smaller birds but also larger birds such as the Australian Magpie. They usually interact in pairs but sometimes gather in large noisy flocks & arrive & depart erratically.

Noisy rainbow lorikeeet
Chatter, chatter, chatter
When you arrive en masse
The silence you do shatter

Noisy rainbow lorikeet
Squabble, squabble, squabble
Squabble over where to perch
Squabble over where to hobble

Noisy rainbow lorikeet
Flutter, flutter, flutter
Your wings never stop
Nor the screeches you utter

Noisy rainbow lorikeet
Colour, colour, colours that delight
When you leave en masse
You're a rainbow in flight

Rain

Rain falling on an Aussie tin roof
Is magic to hear
As it falls softly
It is music to an Aussie ear.

Rain that breaks the Aussie drought
Is God's answer to a desperate farmer's
prayer
Bringing to him elation
To replace overwhelming despair

Rain that soaks the parched, cracked
earth
And fills the dried up dams
Providing life saving water
For the thirsty sheep and lambs

Rain that pounds on an Aussie tin roof
Till it roars like thunder
Is a pleasant way to be woken up
For the Aussies who dwell Downunder

Hidden Danger

The blue ring octopus found in shallow coral and rock pools of Australia is not aggressive if left undisturbed. It is pale brown to yellow in colour and the blue rings on its body only light up as a warning when it feels threatened. It grows from the size of a pea to the size of a golf ball in adulthood. Never pick one up as it carries enough poison to kill 26 adults within minutes.

Rockpools sparkle and glisten
On a nearby rocky shore
Enticing us to linger
Their shallows to explore

In their limpid pristine waters
Myriad aquatic creatures thrive
In this saline watery cosmos
Only the strongest will survive

Corals, seaweeds, anemones and snails
All in it's waters hide
Barnacles, limpets and sea stars
All clinging to its side

But its beauty hides a hidden danger
Of which we all should be aware
It's the deadly, blue ring octopus
Should we accidentally disturb his lair

Print information available on the last page

Rev. date: 08/04/2015

To order additional copies of this book, contact:
Xlibris
1-800-455-039
www.xlibris.com.au
Orders@Xlibris.com.au

Printed in the United States
By Bookmasters